For

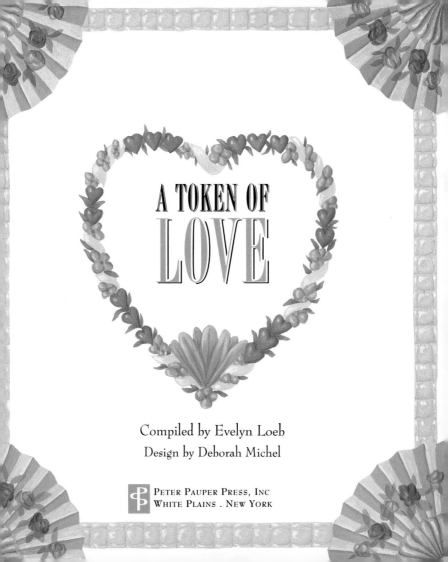

A TOKEN OF
LOVE

Compiled by Evelyn Loeb
Design by Deborah Michel

PETER PAUPER PRESS, INC
WHITE PLAINS . NEW YORK

Copyright © 1994
Peter Pauper Press, Inc.
202 Mamaroneck Avenue
White Plains, NY 10601
All rights reserved
ISBN 0-88088-877-6
Printed in Singapore
7 6 5 4 3 2 1

Jacket background painting by Linda DeVito Soltis
Jacket inset painting by Grace De Vito

CONTENTS

For love
is heaven,
and heaven
is love.

SIR WALTER SCOTT

I Love You in Any Language

China: ♥ Wo ai nei

England: ♥ I love you

France: ♥ Je t'aime

Germany: ♥ Ich liebe dich

Greece: ♥ S'agapo

Hawaii: ♥ Aloha wau ia oe

Ireland: ♥ Thaim in grabh leat

Israel: ♥ Ani ohev otakh

Italy: ♥ Ti amo

Japan: ♥ Ai shite imasu

Spain: ♥ Te amo

Set Me As a Seal

Set me as a seal upon thine heart;
As a seal upon thine arm:
For love is strong as death;
Jealousy is cruel as the grave,
The flashes thereof are flashes of fire,
A very flame of the Lord.
Many waters cannot quench love,
Neither can the floods drown it ...

KING SOLOMON

Love Gods

$\mathcal{T}$he Romans knew her as VENUS, the goddess of love, beauty, and fertility. The Greeks called her APHRODITE, for they believed that she arose from the *aphros* or foam of the sea. Lovely beyond compare, Aphrodite drifted among the Greek Islands before at last reaching the home of the gods on Mount Olympus.

$\mathcal{A}$phrodite immediately entranced Zeus, but when she would not give herself to him, he forced her to marry his lame son Hephaestus, the blacksmith. The marriage was an unhappy one, and Aphrodite indulged in many love affairs. From her most famous liaison, with Ares, the god of war, came five children, including EROS (or CUPID to the Romans), who came to symbolize love.

The most noteworthy of Aphrodite's other attachments was her love of Adonis, the mortal huntsman. Adonis, however, did not return the goddess's affection, but rather preferred the thrill of the hunt. In spite of Aphrodite's warnings to take care, Adonis was killed one day in the woods by a wild boar. His spirit instantly descended to the underworld and into the arms of its queen, Persephone. Heartbroken, Aphrodite appealed to Zeus to bring Adonis back, but by then Persephone also loved Adonis, and asked Zeus to leave the hunter with her.

Zeus, caught between two goddesses, declared in Solomonic fashion that Adonis would spend six months a year with each one. When Adonis resides in the underworld, the earth becomes chilly, then cold and barren, as in autumn and winter, but when he returns above to Aphrodite, her joy transforms the world into the bloom of spring and summer.

Eros, the son of Aphrodite, caused mortals and gods alike to fall irrevocably in love, simply by wounding them with one of his invisible arrows. He can claim credit for the loves of Medea and Jason, Dido's passion for Aeneas, and his own mother's adoration of Adonis. Eros is often depicted as blindfolded, perhaps to explain the often unlikely alliances he induces.

*I*ndeed, even Eros was subject to his own random powers. He accidentally wounded himself with an arrow while on a mission for Aphrodite, and fell in love with the beautiful mortal girl Psyche. Ironically, Aphrodite had wanted Psyche to fall in love with a lowly mortal so that Psyche's beauty would no longer rival her own. Eros, ruled by his passion for Psyche, came to her every night, but in order to guard her from Aphrodite's jealous wrath, never allowed her to see his person in the light. One night, however, overcome by curiosity, Psyche lit a lamp in order to view at last the man she loved.

$\mathcal{A}$stonished by Eros's beauty, Psyche inadvertently spilled a drop of hot oil on him, and awoke him from his slumber. Eros flew away instantly, in spite of his continued love for Psyche, and left her in despair. The lovers were eventually reconciled after Psyche performed three arduous tasks to appease Aphrodite, and Eros convinced Zeus to make Psyche immortal so that they could live together happily forever.

LOVERS' POTPOURRI

*O*ne of the most popular, endearing, and traditional uses of potpourri is to strengthen feelings of love and family togetherness on holidays and at gatherings in the home. At these times, people come together to reflect, share, and rejoice. The use of home-made potpourri can enrich these occasions with visual, scent-filled, and tasty treats.

1 cup rose petals
1 cup rose hips
1/2 cup rosemary leaves
1/2 cup red dianthus blossoms
1/2 cup bachelor's button blossoms and leaves
1 cup honeysuckle flowers
1/2 cup mint leaves (apple mint best)

These herbs and flowers, dried in the summer and autumn, and stored in a closed, dark container, give a whiff of early spring and some lovable whimsy to Valentine's Day. Fragrance evokes what words may fail to express. Give a tin of potpourri filled with your heart's wishes to a friend or loved one. The day will linger, the feelings will have substance.

HEART-SHAPED SUGAR COOKIES

   1/2 cup soft butter
   1/2 cup sugar
   1 egg
   1 tablespoon milk or cream
   1/2 teaspoon vanilla
   1/2 teaspoon lemon extract
   1-1/2 cups flour
   1 teaspoon cream of tartar
   1/2 teaspoon baking soda
   1/4 teaspoon salt

*C*ombine ingredients in above order. Chill dough. Roll out very thin, about 1/8 of an inch. Cut into heart shapes with cookie cutter, sprinkle with red-colored sugar, and bake at 350° on greased cookie sheets until very lightly browned—about 8-10 minutes. Watch carefully to keep from over-browning. One recipe makes about 80 small cookies.

LOVE IS

THOUGHTFUL

17

She Walks in Beauty

She walks in beauty, like the night
  Of cloudless climes and starry skies,
And all that's best of dark and bright
  Meets in her aspect and her eyes,
Thus mellowed to that tender light
  Which heaven to gaudy day denies.

One shade the more, one ray the less
  Had half impaired the nameless grace
Which waves in every raven tress
  Or softly lightens o'er her face,
Where thoughts serenely sweet express
  How pure, how dear their dwelling-place.

And on that cheek and o'er that brow
  So soft, so calm, yet eloquent,
The smiles that win, the tints that glow,

But tell of days in goodness spent,—
A mind at peace with all below,
A heart whose love is innocent.

LORD BYRON

Jenny Kissed Me

Jenny kissed me when we met,
Jumping from the chair she sat in;
Time, you thief, who love to get
Sweets into your list, put that in!
Say I'm weary, say I'm sad,
Say that health and wealth have missed me,
Say I'm growing old, but add,
Jenny kissed me.

LEIGH HUNT

LOVE IS

CONSTANT

$\mathcal{I}$ love you for ignoring the possibilities of the fool and weakling in me, and for laying firm hold on the possibilities of the good in me.

♥

$\mathcal{I}$ love you for closing your ears to the discords in me, and for adding to the music in me by worshipful listening.

♥

$\mathcal{I}$ love you because you are helping me to make of the timber of my life not a tavern, but a temple, and of the words of my every day not a reproach, but a song.

♥

$\mathcal{I}$ love you because you have done more than any creed could have done to make me happy.

$\mathcal{Y}$ou have done it without a touch, without a word, without a sign.

♥

$\mathcal{Y}$ou have done it first by being yourself.

♥

$\mathcal{A}$fter all, perhaps this is what love means.

ANONYMOUS

LOVE ANECDOTES

*W*hen, in 1839, Benjamin Disraeli married the widow Mary Anne Wyndham Lewis, a woman 12 years older than he, he married her fortune and London townhouse as well. The marriage turned out to be a happy one, however—though Disraeli often teased his wife that he had wed her only for her money. "But," she would always answer, "if you had to do it again, you'd do it for love!"

♥

*G*eorge Bernard Shaw was for once taken aback when he appealed to Mrs. Shaw for support of his claim that male judgment was superior to female judgment.

"Of course, dear," replied Mrs. Shaw. "After all, you married me and I you."

Herbal Love Bath

Ingredients:

  1 cup lavender
  1 cup rosemary
  1 cup rose petals
  1/2 cup rose geranium leaves
  1/2 cup lemon verbena leaves
  1 tablespoon each thyme, mint, sage, and orrisroot
   powder

Method:

Combine all ingredients. Mix thoroughly and keep in a tightly lidded container. To make a bath ball, pack 1/4 cup in a muslin square and tie securely. Bring to a boil in 1 cup of water and let stand for 10 minutes. Add the bath ball to hot bath water and use it to scrub yourself. Relax in the bath and let your thoughts focus on romance.

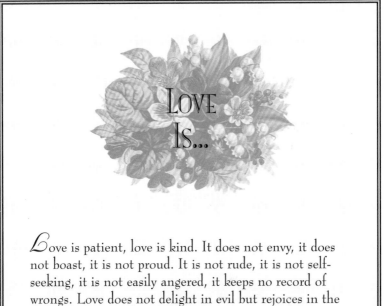

LOVE IS...

$\mathcal{L}$ove is patient, love is kind. It does not envy, it does not boast, it is not proud. It is not rude, it is not self-seeking, it is not easily angered, it keeps no record of wrongs. Love does not delight in evil but rejoices in the truth. It always protects, always trusts, always hopes, always perseveres.

Love never fails.

I CORINTHIANS 13:1-8 (NIV)

LOVE IS

KIND

28

Love is saying you're sorry and meaning it.

♥

Love is accepting an apology wholeheartedly.

♥

Love is making the coffee before your beloved awakens.

♥

Love is sending flowers for no reason.

♥

Love is wanting only the best for that special someone.

♥

Love is letting him watch football when you'd
rather watch a great movie.

Love is going shopping with her until she's ready to quit.

♥

Love is sharing the household chores.

♥

Love is never closing the door unless it's the bathroom.

♥

Love is putting your dirty clothing into the hamper.

♥

Love is being aware of that new haircut or dress.

CONSUMING PASSIONS

*T*he sweet mystery of aphrodisiacs is as old as civilization itself. Judeo-Christian tradition links the fall of Adam and Eve directly to their consumption of the Fruit of Knowledge.

*H*istory is rife with references to love potions derived from foods. From the Garden of Eden to modern times, people of all nations have ascribed special amatory properties to some of the most basic edibles. Just as the plants in a garden need an occasional helping of fertilizer, so too do people need an occasional stimulatory boost to heighten sexual desire.

$\mathcal{A}$phrodisiacs fall into different categories based on their different stimulatory properties and histories. Some, such as wheat and rice, derive their love potion status from strongly-held beliefs about their power to enhance fertility. The tradition of tossing rice at a wedding stems from this ancient notion. Thus, the couple at whom it is tossed will quickly bear new life. Other aphrodisiacs, like oysters and figs, derive their mystical powers from what many perceive as their physical likeness to male and/or female sex organs. Other foods are believed to enhance sexual potency because of their composition of minerals, such as bananas, which

are rich in potassium, a mineral essential for the healthy function of the muscles and nerves.

And yet there are other aphrodisiacs whose status grew from age-old traditions and practices which have spanned the generations. The word *honeymoon* was coined in Ancient Europe, where newlyweds were thought to derive their unflagging lust from drinking honey wine; thus honey's status as one of the most exalted aphrodisiacs in history. And ever since the Kama Sutra proclaimed the penis-enlarging power of pomegranates, they too have ripened into a leader among a host of other purported potions. But what would our list amount to without the most beloved of all aphrodisiacs— chocolate? If you think you have an insatiable desire for the sweet, consider Aztec Emperor Moctezuma II, who was known to drink no less than fifty glasses of it a day, plus an extra goblet or two prior to sex!

*I*n the following recipes, we have included some of the most enduring aphrodisiacs—chocolate, honey, pomegranates, oysters, figs and bananas. If you make each dish with love, care, and (most of all) an open mind, you just might reap some of the most blissful rewards!

Bon Appetit!

LOVE IS

GIVING

36

OYSTERS ROCKEFELLER

36 oysters on the half shell
Rock salt
2 cups cooked and drained spinach
1/4 cup chopped scallions
2 tablespoons minced parsley
2 tablespoons finely chopped celery
1/2 teaspoon salt
6 drops hot pepper sauce
1/3 cup butter
2 teaspoons anisette
1/2 cup fine dry bread crumbs

$\mathscr{P}$ut oysters in their shells on a bed of rock salt so they will remain upright and not lose their juice. Combine spinach, scallions, parsley, and celery. Put this mixture through a food grinder. Add salt and hot pepper sauce, mixing well.

Cook mixture in butter and anisette over low heat for 4 or 5 minutes. Fold in bread crumbs and spread 1 tablespoon of mixture on each oyster. Bake in a 400° oven for 10 minutes or until lightly browned.

CHOCOLATE TRUFFLES

3/4 cup heavy cream
8 ounces semisweet or dark sweet chocolate,
    coarsely chopped
2 tablespoons dark rum, brandy, Amaretto,
    or other liqueur (optional)

CHOICE OF COATINGS:
    Unsweetened cocoa
    Chocolate sprinkles
    Finely chopped almonds, pecans, or walnuts

*P*lace cream in medium size heavy saucepan. Cook
over moderate heat just until bubbles begin to form
around edges of cream. Add chocolate and cook, stirring,
about 2 minutes. Remove from heat and continue
stirring until chocolate is completely melted. Cool to
room temperature and stir in liqueur. Spoon into bowl,

cover loosely with waxed paper, and place in refrigerator at least 2 hours or until thickened, stirring occasionally.

Line cookie sheet with waxed paper. Dust hands lightly with confectioners sugar or cocoa. Form chocolate mixture into 1-inch balls and place balls on lined cookie sheet. Place cookie sheet, uncovered, in refrigerator at least ten minutes or until truffles are firm.

Line second cookie sheet with waxed paper and set aside. One coating may be used for all truffles or a variety of coatings may be used. Place each coating on separate piece of waxed paper and roll truffles gently in coating. Place coated truffles on freshly lined cookie sheet and return to refrigerator, uncovered, until firm.

When truffles are firm, place in miniature paper cups, if desired, and place between layers of waxed paper in

LOVE IS

SWEET

tightly covered container. Store in refrigerator. About 2 dozen truffles.

HINTS AND TIPS:

Unwanted moisture can cause disaster when working with chocolate. Use dry utensils, *never* cover a pan in which chocolate is being melted, and don't try to make truffles on a rainy or humid day. Even as little as one drop of water can cause chocolate to stiffen.

Chocolate should be melted over low or moderate heat. High heat will cause chocolate to burn.

Traditionally, unsweetened cocoa is used to coat truffles. If you find the flavor of unsweetened cocoa too bitter, be untraditional and use sweetened cocoa instead.

The quality and flavor of a truffle are directly related to the quality of chocolate used. Buy the very best quality chocolate you can afford.

BARBARA BLOCH

Honey-Date Cake

2-1/2 cups all-purpose flour
1/2 cup firmly packed light brown sugar
1 teaspoon baking powder
1 teaspoon baking soda
1 teaspoon cinnamon
1/4 teaspoon salt
3 eggs, beaten
1 cup honey
1/2 cup strong black coffee
1/4 cup vegetable oil
1 cup chopped, pitted dates
Walnut halves to decorate

*P*reheat oven to 350°. Lightly grease and flour 9 x 9-inch square pan and set aside.

Place flour, sugar, baking powder, baking soda, cinnamon, and salt in large bowl and stir until well combined. Make well in center and stir in eggs, honey, coffee, and oil. Stir until smooth and well combined. Stir in dates.

Pour into prepared pan and arrange nuts on top of batter. Bake in preheated oven about 45 to 55 minutes or until toothpick inserted in center comes out clean.

Cool in pan on wire rack 10 minutes. Remove from pan and cool completely on wire rack. Cut into squares to serve.

BARBARA BLOCH

Banana-Nut Bread

1-3/4 cups all-purpose flour
3/4 cup sugar
1-1/2 teaspoons baking powder
1/2 teaspoon baking soda
1/2 teaspoon salt
1/2 teaspoon ginger
1/4 teaspoon nutmeg
1/4 teaspoon allspice
1 teaspoon grated lemon peel
1/2 cup butter, softened
2 eggs, beaten
1-1/2 cups mashed ripe bananas
3/4 cup coarsely chopped pecans

$\mathcal{P}$reheat oven to 350°. Lightly grease and flour 9 x 5-inch loaf pan and set aside.

Sift flour, sugar, baking powder, baking soda, salt, ginger, nutmeg, and allspice into large bowl. Stir in lemon peel. Add butter and cut into flour mixture with pastry blender or 2 knives until mixture resembles coarse crumbs. Stir in eggs and mashed bananas until well blended. Stir in nuts.

Pour into prepared pan and bake in preheated oven about 1 hour or until toothpick inserted in center comes out clean.

Cool in pan on wire rack 10 minutes. Remove from pan and cool completely on wire rack.

BARBARA BLOCH

POMEGRANATE-KIWIFRUIT DELIGHT

Per portion:

1 pomegranate
1 scoop ice cream (any flavor)
1/2 to 1 kiwifruit, peeled and sliced

Remove blossom end of pomegranate carefully and score skin gently with tip of knife to quarter fruit. Break fruit open gently along score lines to open pomegranate like a flower. Place on service plate, place scoop of ice cream in center of fruit, and garnish with slices of kiwifruit.

TIP: If desired, remove seeds from pomegranate after it has been opened. Seeds add delicious crunch to salad dressings.

BARBARA BLOCH

LOVE IS

DELIGHT

Southern Fig Preserves

3-1/2 cups sugar
About 24 fresh, firm figs (2 to 2-1/2 pounds)
1 large lemon, sliced and pitted

$\mathcal{P}$lace sugar in heavy 3-quart saucepan. Stir in 3 cups water and bring to a boil. Reduce heat slightly and cook, stirring, until sugar has been completely dissolved. Rinse figs thoroughly under cold running water and add to saucepan with lemon slices. Cook, uncovered, about 30 minutes until figs are translucent. Stir occasionally and add water as necessary if syrup gets too thick.

Cool fig preserves and store in covered container in refrigerator or spoon into hot sterilized jars and process 30 minutes in hot-water bath.

Serve with Baking Powder Biscuits or as a side dish with ham or tongue.

BARBARA BLOCH

Traditional Anniversary Gifts

Year

One ♥ Paper

Two ♥ Cotton

Three ♥ Leather

Four ♥ Flowers

Five ♥ Wood

Six ♥ Candy

Seven ♥ Copper

Eight ♥ Bronze

Nine ♥ Pottery

Ten ♥ Tin

Eleven ♥ Steel
Twelve ♥ Silk
Thirteen ♥ Lace
Fourteen ♥ Ivory
Fifteen ♥ Crystal
Twenty ♥ China
Twenty-Five ♥ Silver
Thirty ♥ Pearl
Thirty-Five ♥ Coral
Forty ♥ Ruby
Forty-Five ♥ Sapphire
Fifty ♥ Gold
Fifty-Five ♥ Emerald
Sixty ♥ Diamond

To Celia

Drink to me only with thine eyes
And I will pledge with mine
Or leave a kiss but in the cup
And I'll not look for wine.
The thirst that from the soul doth rise
Doth ask a drink divine
But might I of Jove's nectar sup
I would not change for thine.

I sent thee late a rosy wreath,
Not so much honoring thee
As giving it a hope that there
It could not withered be.
But thou thereon didst only breathe
And send'st it back to me:
Since when it grows, and smells, I swear,
Not of itself but thee.

BEN JONSON

How Do I Love Thee?

How do I love thee? Let me count the ways.
I love thee to the depth and breadth and height
My soul can reach, when feeling out of sight
For the ends of Being and ideal Grace.
I love thee to the level of everyday's
Most quiet need, by sun and candle-light.
I love thee freely, as men strive for Right;
I love thee purely, as they turn from Praise.
I love thee with the passion put to use
In my old griefs, and with my childhood's faith.
I love thee with a love I seemed to lose
With my lost saints,—I love thee with the breath,
Smiles, tears, of all my life!—and, if God choose,
I shall but love thee better after death.

ELIZABETH BARRETT BROWNING

LOVE IS

FREE